A Handful of Blue Earth

A Handful of Blue Earth

Vénus Khoury-Ghata

Translated from the French
by Marilyn Hacker

from
Le Livre des suppliques (Mercure de France 2015)
and
La Dame de Syros (Collection Ekphrasis, 2012)

First published 2017 by
Liverpool University Press
4 Cambridge Street
Liverpool
L69 7ZU

Copyright © 2017 Liverpool University Press

Translated with permision from:
Le Livre des suppliques © Mercure de France, 2015
Les Dame de Syros © Vénus Khoury-Ghata, 2012

The right of Vénus Khoury-Ghata to be identified as the author of this book has been asserted by her in accordance with the Copyright, Designs and Patents Act 1988.

The right of Marilyn Hacker to be identified as the author of the preface and translator of this book has been asserted by her in accordance with the Copyright, Designs and Patents Act 1988.

All rights reserved. No part of this book may be reproduced, stored in a retrieval system, or transmitted, in any form or by any means, electronic, mechanical, photocopying, recording, or otherwise, without the prior written permission of the publisher.

British Library Cataloguing-in-Publication data
A British Library CIP record is available

ISBN 978-1-78694-011-7 softback

Typeset by Carnegie Book Production, Lancaster
Printed and bound in Poland by Booksfactory.co.uk

Contents

Preface	vii
The Lady of Syros	1
from *The Book of Petitions*	17
The Mothers and the Mediterranean	41
Acknowledgments	55

Preface

Vénus Khoury-Ghata was born in Bcharré, a Christian village in northern Lebanon. Raised in Beirut, she was not the child of the intelligentsia like many literary émigrés, but one of four children of a bilingual policeman and a practical-nurse-turned-housewife. She has lived in France since 1972.

Although her mother tongue (and her mother's tongue) is Arabic, Khoury-Ghata has become a major figure in Francophone writing, the literature of writers from the Maghreb, the Middle East, sub-Saharan Africa, Canada, the West Indies, who, as the Algerian playwright and poet Kateb Yacine memorably stated, "write in French to tell the French that I am not French". They bring to the French of France a poetry rich in narrative, fantasy, satire and engagement.

A prolific writer of fiction as well as poetry, Vénus Khoury-Ghata has published twenty novels and eighteen collections of poems. After settling in France, she chose French as her language of expression. She herself translates contemporary Arabic poetry, especially that of the Syro-Lebanese poet Adonis. The Arabic language seems to speak through her French, in her elaborate, pithy figurative language, in the word-play possible in a language where one "root" gives rise to myriad words, in the landscapes and seasons through which her poems' protagonists (hers *are* poems with protagonists) move.

The first sequence of the present book is exphrastic, in the voice of a Cycladic statue "the lady of Syros," yet "her" story merges with some obsessive themes of Khoury-Ghata's poetry and fiction: the death of a brother closer than a twin; an enforced silence at once erotic and oppressive, and a female protagonist's reclamation of her own narrative.

The rest of the book is from the author's most recent collection, *Le Livre des suppliques*, published in 2015, written after the death of the poet's life partner, a decorated hero of the Resistance decades earlier, stepfather to the poet's youngest daughter—Yasmine Ghata, now herself a novelist—after her husband's death. But the addressee of the wry elegies in "The Book of Petitions" has little to do with the actual man mourned. As in a much earlier poem, "The Dead Man's Monologue," death becomes a kind of departure into exile, expatriation to a country with captious laws, a bad postal service, a close, uneasy relation to the world of animals and plants.

"The Mothers and the Mediterranean" also abounds with surreal images, and loquacity after death, but it is a sequence about contemporary urban warfare, where the border between combatant and civilian is as porous as that between victim and survivor. Today, the city is Aleppo, Mosul, Manama … but here it is Beirut, not now in the centre of a combat zone, reimagined as it was during the not-forgotten civil war, blending into contemporary conflicts.

Khoury-Ghata's poem sequences are exploded narratives, re-assembled in a mosaic or labyrinth in which the reader, like Ariadne, finds a connecting thread. Themes which also animate her fiction recur in the poems: the tension between movement/ change and tradition/ sources, with all that is positive and negative in both; the unceasing commerce between humans and the rest of the natural world, between the dead and the living; the independent, puissant, transcultural life of languages and of words.

The Lady of Syros

I

He drills through the rock, drills through the day
in a vertical line in his sleep

Woodpecker's beak or pickaxe
he located my grave
digs with regular incisive blows
spits on his sore palms
stops to catch his breath, pants

This man keeps a forge in his chest
why this determination to unearth me
when real gods proliferate underground
crippled, one-armed, disfigured, all they want
    is to climb back on their pedestals

Pickaxe, shovel, chisel, brush
he changes tools the closer he comes to me
    and the sun turns its back on him
rubble and dust brushed away
with his two hands he gently parts the earth
like the sex of a prepubescent girl

He is terrified of scratching me
of cracking my body turned stony
    with so much silence

Pickaxe, chisel, shovels put down
he speaks to me through silica, sand, pebbles, recalcitrant
    roots
urges me to emerge before nightfall, before the wolves
the real owners of this island

What does this man who speaks with his tools want of me?
His hands cry out when his mouth is silent
he is not a grave robber or a looter of tombs
    he is searching for amulets
    and buried statues

Last call for the boat back to the mainland
he won't leave before he has freed me
from my coat of stone
a silence four thousand five hundred years long
    beside a dead queen, buried with her jewels
silence crossed by an earthquake
    a thousand years later
Santorini, Delos, Chios, Syros lifted by the sea
crumbled like a poor man's bread
given to the fire to eat

Dried between two layers of earth I felt all the noise
    but pretended not to hear

II

Shut in with the dead
I adopted their indifference
    to what was outside

The living were no friends of ours
they accused us of throwing stones
    into their sleep
of howling with wolves and echoes
of hindering the rivers' flow although
    we'd never pushed ahead of the smallest stream
they said we were rooted though we moved
    from burial plot to burial plot with our load
    of crumbling bones
that we were what no longer was
identical only to ourselves
reversible in rainy or in humble weather

The freshly painted newcomers
    looked at us with disdain
incapable of informing us
    about what we had become
if we were habitable or inhabited

III

Dead yet desired by the man
    who kept on digging
the archaeologist's laughter ripples down his chest
    at the sight of my foot
his laughter reaches the sun and the only star
    visible at this hour

He lifts me like a goatskin full of fresh water
looks me over from head to feet
62 centimetres long and 5 centimetres wide
marble chiseled in marble
wets me with saliva so he can see
    my original colour
dries me with his shirt-tail
is enraptured by the purity of my stone
    and how it resisted burial
fascinated by my narrow loins
by my unscathed limbs
a little clay and know-how will fill
    the two nicks in the groin and the right foot

Once the boat has left for the mainland
and Syros is given back to the jackals
he spreads a jute sack on the ground ready to spend
    the night in my company

Why does he ask me my name when
    my ears are sealed
why does he wait on my answer when
    I have no mouth

The nose that divides my face is the only feature given me by the old sculptor who took me in when I was wandering in search of my twin brother gone to live on the invisible side of the earth the mother said

IV

The old sculptor of Syros carved me
    according to his own needs
mute so as not to contradict him
arms crossed on my chest to avoid all embraces
thighs sealed shut to preserve my virginity
eyes were superfluous
the old sculptor of Syros was blind

Gaze turned inward
legs fettered, arms sealed to the chest
    the girl sculpted by the man whose eyelids were sewn shut
    with iron thread
The dead princess I was meant to accompany
    to the other world had nothing to say
it was yesterday it was very long ago
thousands and thousands of years
I still hear my mother's voice as she brought in
    the laundry hung between two cypress trees
"Come back to the house, Kia, the death that took
    your brother away doesn't want you!"
Her voice crossed out by the angrily blowing wind
a subterranean wind that cracked the earth
raised the waves and made ships
    pitch in the cove
wind that announced a storm

V

It was yesterday
a thousand and a thousand years ago
I was watching the horizon
place where the dead gather
    those vagabonds

I had to stride across the sea to find
    my twin my equal my brother
my mother's voice sailed above Santorini
    sailed above Chios
seen from afar, Syros looked like a chessboard
    white and black

Syros, Santorini, Delos, Chios, magma of lava
    mud and polluted water a thousand years later
the din reached me in my dark den of a world
    another world had pushed away
    and I rejoiced
a cataclysm meant for those who live above
those who live below are sheltered between two stones

The archaeologist who just unearthed me
    didn't know the man who sculpted me
didn't know my mother or the colour of her voice
nor the sorrow of our two linden trees
    when my brother's body was carried past
nor the way their leaves applauded
    when the procession disappeared

The archaeologist who excavates the island knows only me
placed on his burly chest
he gives me the tree's movements
    to unfetter my arms
the cry of water in a pitcher
    to quench my millennial thirst
the odour of bread to give me a mouth
the clatter of metal bowls to spread
    my frightened girlish thighs

VI

Tomorrow
but only in his mind
he'll draw me eyelashes
glue hair to my skull
will sew me a tunic to measure
    and thong sandals for my narrow feet

Tomorrow
the archaeologist will announce his discovery to the four
    winds
will describe me as a Cycladic idol possessed
    of great powers
alive despite all appearances
with knowledge surpassing that
    of the pebbles on the roads
he will read the holes in my torso
an alphabet of wishes and regret
although only the wind could write at that time
it wrote and erased the sentences scribbled
    on the un-margined pages of the sea

My arms crossed on myself
I am my own cage
at once prison and prisoner

VII

Face without a face
nose sniffing out the dead wrapped tight in their bandages
my silent silhouette reigned
    over all the necropolis

The sculptor from Syros wanted it
he had pruned me like a sick tree
carved away what was superfluous to my survival
erased my surplus temporality
kept the invisible cry
the frozen gaze turned inwards

He enclosed me in a space defined for all time
clothed in nudity
I wore my body inside out waiting
    for an unforeseeable ceremony

VIII

The sculptor of Syros wanted me slender
    as a stake
silent as clay
immobile in my bones
arms crossed on the threshold of the infinite
Woman or statue, what's the difference!

With a liquefied face
the slit of my womb sealed shut
    the sculptor of Syros wanted me

The dead don't desire each other
don't penetrate each other
useless to engender more dead

The earth, filled to the brim, barricaded its door

Let the surplus ones bury themselves with their own hands
    in a hole in the air

Closed in between two layers of earth
I could draw the world without moving my hand
movements borrowed from disused beings
I sketched a creek from the crashing
    of the backwash on the rocks
a grove of trees from the wind's noise as it pulled
    the branches' hair
city streets from wooden clogs trampling
    the tender and the dry
Dead, I recognised trees by their odour
acrid for the jujube tree
bitter for the cypress
acid, the elder-tree that grows in cemeteries

IX

The crumbled voice of my mother crying
"Come back! The death that carried off your brother
    doesn't want you!"
Was she talking to me or to the boy buried on
    the hill whose odour tempted jackals and wolves?

"Come back, and we'll give you quails to eat
    stuffed with Smyrna grapes
bread as white as the first snowfall
wine made from rubies' blood
a bed of virgin wool tied at the ends
Come back and we'll carry on our shoulders
    the noise of your burial."

Twenty pickaxes go to work around your head
Twenty women throw their veils into the hole
Twenty necessary words to loose you
    from your outdated shell
and offer you a garment that suits you
a carrier pigeon's
or the beast's that even vultures fear

"Where are you going like that?" the mother cried as
    I went with the stream as far as the river
and with the river to the sea
"Come back! The river is big enough
    to know its own way
Bring your footsteps back in your shoes
Bring the house back to the house"

X

I walked for three days and three nights
one foot on the bank and one in the stream
the hostile buzzing of bees in my ears
and the bones' dry buzzing in the cemetery
I walked in my death
pacing its underside for thousands of years
    without going forward

Gravedigger bird or pickaxe
pecks at the earth
empties it from within
strains the clay through his hands
"Make a place for me beside you!"

The archaeologist's laughter flows down his chest
    like an untouched waterfall

from *The Book of Petitions*

Whether it's true or false
We said to ourselves that you would continue to play dead by omission or out of laziness to distinguish you from those who walk with their backs to the city's noise that you'd offer us a bottle of sherry to celebrate the coming of a winter clad in Afghan goat's wool and boots gathered in the tombs of the rich.
Whether it's true or false
We also said to ourselves that your walled-up voice would be able to decide among us when it came to the distribution of winds in the plane-tree on the square, and to train the fireflies escaped from the sleeves of darkness to light up God's road when he came alone to check the content of his snow, and to see if passers-by slipped on his tears when he suddenly felt like weeping.

Must you be reminded that you are only what is said and
    forgotten
brother of shadows calling out in the chestnut tree
sketched thought
silence chipped away by use
that the wind pushing you toward the pond is not the pond's
    friend, nor the friend of the washerwomen who wring
    you out with the red linens of women in childbirth, who
    complain of pebbles in their chests as their arms fall when
    night does
when their arms drop with darkness

Let's admit that your disappearance was a pretence
staged in complicity with the eclipse of a comic sun
that you never went far from the doorstep where you made
    holes in the sky with your slingshot killing angels and
    bluejays with one blow
only imaginary the feathers that bloodied the grey woman's
    hair
how to know who plucked the angel's feathers and ate the
    bluejay
and that what happened, happened

Let's admit that you made a bad decision
Having chosen walls with a view of other walls is no reason
    to speak ill of the snails in the garden and the grass that
    doesn't remember your name
Not the slightest echo of your consultations with the
    blackbird who had a crush on himself
becoming two blackbirds in the bay window
No sign either of an eventual sketch of your face
the steam rising from the soup is the image of no known soul
The woman standing facing the sink makes the faucet cry

You watch for the moment when dusk makes its way to your table to write down its tall tales
Dust unto dust, the words it dictates to you
Disappointment weighs down your shoulders
Why were you called to this earth if your fingers dilute the messages meant for you
Slumped on the suddenly darkened page
you tell yourself that writing is the invention of a deaf-mute alphabet,
Words don't cry out in protest at the end of the man who was writing

The faces lined up on the walls invite you to join them
their comments make the plaster sweat
The beggar must take off his shoes before crossing the
 threshold
The hunter must hang his game-bag on the walnut tree
and the women hold back their tears that would catch fire
 touching your forehead

when you think about it
your death has not aged your house or whitened the hair of
 the walnut tree that always looks straight into the sun
 despite its bitter fruit and its nest's frayed straw
a beating of wings like applause
that's all that you take away
only the sooty-winged lark will wear mourning for you

A handful of red earth for your shoulder that protected you
    from the storm
a handful of blue earth for the one that bore your sorrows
a last one for the sparrow that announces your burial to the
    trees in the forest

Deprived of any ceremony
your chair and your bed still have something to say about the
    way you drove a nail into bare wood
joined the angles
smoothed the wood by hand the way you'd stroke a pet

This hole in the ground is incomprehensible to your
    possessions,
They are convinced that everything that breathes and sweats
    ends up on the garbage dump

Everything speaks to you of departure
Words squirm around on the page
the man walking under a rainstorm brushes you with his
    thoughts
you feel the dampness of his feet in your calves
You are you and all the passers-by at once
the keys of their houses jangle in your pockets
you open walls and doors
None of them are like yours that grew old while you went off
    following these strangers
their rain-slicked hair accuses you of negligence
If you were more responsible you'd have lined them up on
    your windowsill
dried their feet alongside the herbs from your garden
and played out the scene in the opposite sense
inching your way into the people walking to make up for your
    own inertia

The stones in your garden speak louder than the people
    passing by
they claim an ancestry that goes back to the first cave
when two flintstones controlled fire
and a pauper wind swept the brambles of an alphabet gone
    deaf

Things being what they were
you had only to grasp a stone in your hand to feel the planet's
    vibrations
sense a volcano's insurrection
the cry of a mountain collapsed by an ant

Hold back your hand when the sunset draws its last circle on
    your wall
the sun is not a drum
and the discussion between darkness and asphalt doesn't
    concern you while your shadow follows you by a finger
    and an eye
You walk and your destinations print themselves on your feet

Water down your anger when the river squats on your
    doormat
a river can't be wrung out
or kicked to chase it away
a river isn't a dog
don't block its path when it steps across your threshold
its water will erase the footprints of the winds come to beg at
    your door
quench the thirst of your hearth
and make your daughters' knees shine like pebbles in a stream

Shame on your wife who has it drink from a bowl riddled
    with holes
it knows her secrets
knows the cleft flesh of her stock-pot and the hairy skin of
    her hemp
shame on you for taking stones from the tired walls of a
    collapsed house to build elsewhere

The poplar tree's scrawniness goes well with your new silhouette
Less fettered and hindered
you would push away the winter with both hands to see if your skin was a continuation of its bark
You think you're applauding the dancing leaves' performance
as you follow the meanderings of shadow in the interstices

You call out as from the bottom of a well when a saw begins its work above you
The man's laughter comes back up to your knees

You are destitute before the sparrows that attack your fig tree
   and unsteady your ladder
Measuring an earth below the earth uses up all your energy

You ask for a chair to put your skeleton back in shape and
for a gap in space so you can find your fig tree
Though you've only the right to the rustling of its leaves
and the acrid odour of its milk

The itinerary of your return in a sewn-up pocket

The one who breaks into the sick garden makes the sick birch tree bleed pale blood
You set fire to the page when you colour in red the hair of the girl who turns her back on the ailing garden
Smoke tarnishes the lamp's brightness
Evening darkens the walls' moods
What you think is a roof is only suspended rain
Undecided souls, laundry trembling in the wind

Tomorrow
the page will stop being a page and the pencil snatched up by the sun will crumble at your feet

What does it matter if you're there where you are not
a tree upside down
or a tiger crossed out by its rage ?
Loose stones have split your toe like a mule's hoof
like the nail of a clumsy shoemaker
The swallow flying above you can't read your marble like
    coffee-grounds,
or read your face in three dimensions

The dead man, she says, is not the one you think

The shovels peeling away the world's underside make no
 distinction
between broken glass   pebbles   bones
you trust the arms that wield them
the mouths that gulp down the planet's most intimate waters
tear it asunder to bury hands and tools

Seen from afar
those men camped on two lands at once
spread their legs like a compass so as not to be snatched up
by the great all
that is nothing

Who will find lost time
who will tie it to the foot of the bed
who will hoist it up on the horse that gallops in four
    directions at once

You ask the most ignorant wind your questions
the one who mistakes a bulrush in your garden for a tardy
    visitor
the sound of the storm on the roof for a quarrel between
    pigeons

Cantankerous wind
that refuses to sit down at table with you for a frank
    discussion
to share your soup
or go back to the turbulent road that dropped it on your
    threshold

How to make it understand that the drainpipe is better than
    the cat-flap for coming into your house?

The woman whom you joined in bed belonged to you
And the cracked jug was yours too
And the river with no water

Seated on the bank as if it were the world's end
you told the toad to sing and the toad sang louder than the rain's drums
You told the wind to chase the smoke from your roof
and the wind drove away the smoke
and the woman hatching a fire between her thighs

There you are pulling your house behind you slowly like a camel

The woman who wasn't in the photo taps her thigh
and the wind bends its neck for the leash
curls up under the table next to the dog who becomes a wolf
    when night stripes the panes
The wolf, she says
is only a wolf by hearsay and gossip
he doesn't trample the young grass
doesn't mock widows in their dresses of grief
An angel before
and a beast behind
the wolf was a bell-ringer in the age of cathedrals
a pilgrim with hairy knees
who stole weathervanes
His disappearance from books leaves her inconsolable

It's winter in her photographs
The silence is cold enough to split a rock
She rubs her hands on the walls to create a little heat
counts them in both directions to have the impression of
    being rich
leafs through her garden like a book adding words of her own
    invention
and a pair of pruning shears for the dead man to trim the
    laurel tree that grew askew

The woman who went down the mountain on her bottom
   brushes off the thorns and silent insects clinging to her
   skirts
She's brought back no clouds on the way, only the odour of
   ewes
And the wool needed to stuff her lover's pillow

Seven seasons waiting for him to come back with the mattress
Seven contortions to get to the centre and that odour of
   underground grass breathed in down to the last whiff
When her cry distended the walls

The fog spit out by the river ends up in the dump
Lame chair wilted flowers broken umbrella go from door to door but no one wants them
The soul of the dead servant hangs laundry out on the line
Her breasts are two magnolia petals
Her dress a stain of misunderstanding
The black cross on the steeple thinks it's a weather-vane
Its turning corresponds to no direction
How can you mark the compass-points when the earth never stops moving?

How can you weep in a language no longer your own
what can you call walls not imbued with your sweat

With your back against the closed door, you invoke the spirit
    of the place to keep away souls whose suffering is pending
    and coyotes
The key is under a stone analogous to all stones
you grope for the riverbed, to sleep there, and the sheets
    stretched between the banks
what stone to lift without panicking the lizards and scattering
    the fearful populace of ants
you know the wind can be no help to you
angry with the water
the well it has been digging for centuries is filled with your
    voice

The Mothers and the Mediterranean

Destroy everything cried the mothers from their high balconies
wring the streetlights' necks
make the trees eat dust
dismember the ladder the doll the spider's hammock
The children will play with the Sea
they will learn addition from the corpses piled on the sidewalks
subtraction from decapitated trees

**

An eye plucked up from the dust for a pistachio ice cream cone for a glass of hibiscus juice--
the merchant on the Corniche trades in everything that can be bought and sold

Tanks crossed the Mediterranean
The mothers called the dead and the children to come in before the bombardments
wept on their balconies and on the shoulder of the rain that rained no longer
green hands plucked the basil that startled at every explosion
stuffed the children

**

Only feathered creatures survive said the mothers
who knitted wings for the children
then pushed them off the balcony railings
Fly, my child
my love
light of my eyes
gathered them up from the asphalt with bruised hearts
replanted them in the garden at the foot of the sorrel that
    cured colic and calmed fears
Fly into the sun
you'll be a hummingbird when you're ten
a red sparrowhawk feared by the storm when hair grows on
    your palms
fly through air and blood and you'll become a sniper

**

The man who fixed pedestrians in his gun-sights
followed the sun's trajectory
his laughter splattered the blood of the sunset

Planning his night in the evening
his fists cried out on single women's doors
the omelette wolfed down standing
he returned to his roof
begged the rain to dilute him to a timid boy
with a diaphanous mother and a grassy house
his name on a cup hanging over the kitchen sink

**

A relic
the piece of shrapnel rubbed against his jeans
return to the innocence of daisy petals
You love me a little
A lot
Till death…
Tom Thumb's pebbles are the bones unearthed from the sand-pit
washed with no fuss or tears
since everything was dry
rain and hearts alike

**

The jasmine's white odour makes the fighter kneeling at the base of the wall stagger
His machine gun has the soft skin of women with milky breasts
His thickened blood cries out at his legs' intersection
The red hole in the forehead of the old woman looking for her cat makes him fall down laughing
She got what she deserved
cats don't go to war
Cats and old people indoors
killers outdoors
The country belongs to them

**

Napping in the shadow of his cart
the fruit and vegetable man sleeps with his face against the ground
The bombardments startle his cherries but leave him like marble
When the war is over he'll have his own cherry tree
a wife just for himself, and children fresh as magnolia petals
white as a communion wafer

**

After death, there is nothing
fog on fog
and snow on snow
time in circles
cried a cadaver
But no one believed him
The streetlights panicked to see him walking
The palm trees' hair turned white all at once
A train lay down on the tracks
The old woman who liked to see people die declared him an impostor and the market gardener whose orchard he crossed hung himself from a tomato plant
A time to work the earth and a time to rest in it declared the market gardener
cucumbers plump as babies' fingers
green peas round as dimples
beans gleaming like earrings
The recipes the mothers exchange made the bomb shelter's walls water

**

The widow who feeds her dead man loukoums and ginger
   speaks to him in the stopped clock
Take me with you wherever you are
skylight of my eyes
grass of my heart
padlock of my house
Say those words again that ripped the mattress and made the
   pillow fly away
words of crystal and smoke
the clock is no telltale and the sniper on the roof thinks
   you've gone to America

**

Shaking out a sheet over the window railing chased away the
   sniper and the sun
tapping on the cat's bowl made him feel full
The widow on the floor above the floors walked on her tears
   to cool her burned feet
her footprint a five-leafed clover
A good omen decided the gull standing on his rock
the war will be over before the Mediterranean retreats
   completely

**

The Mediterranean took advantage of the widows' slumber to
    retreat as far as Nicosia
The children who saw it leaving didn't hold it back
the wings on their little shoulders keep them from running

Who are you to steal my sunlight? a boy cried out
The sniper, who only fears dogs' barking
took the child apart piece by piece
ranged him in his rucksack, and slept the sleep of the just

**

Long life to you, sniper, son of the virgin and the carpenter
who can tell the useful from the futile
save us from boredom
save the country from peace
cried a madman from his cell
The madman's words ran in the streets
Their harsh accent rasped skin from the trees
made the waves bristle, ruffled the gull's feathers

**

Minuscule in his gun-sight the sniper's house
his mother a moving point on the threshold
broom raised on her sleeve, the jujube tree stripped of its
    leaves
The odour of mechoui with cumin makes the air stagger
lamb chopped parsley shallots
The sniper would trade his kalashnikov for a pinch of love
    and cumin

**

The girl in his gun-sights had walked on his shadow
The explosion tore dress and chest apart
The sniper will follow her funeral from his rooftop
three salvos fired into the air when they lower the coffin
will tear holes in three clouds, and make the air bleed

Tomorrow
the sniper will break his kalashnikov on his knee like a straw
Tomorrow
he'll exchange his life for a plate of lentils with cumin
and a glass of arak

**

In the bomb shelter
there is talk of an army of trees ready to invade the country
wood-chips fierce with men and bark
they will climb the women and the ladders
plant green children at the hips' intersection
will smoke the beehive till the queen is burnt to ashes
dismember men and drones

**

A time of abstinence, austerity
fingers grown so thin their rings fall off
The widows who stir up the depths of the sea with sticks
exhume silent algae and discontented drowned men
the separated husbands are driven back toward the open sea
their wrinkled skin pleads against them
and what seemed to be a diamond is salt petrified between
    two eyelashes
There are too many drowned men to count

**

Tired of wringing out their mops in the Mediterranean
the widows sleep against the walls
sleep on their own shoulders
the candle on the threshold chases off the unwanted dead
    man

Meowing of cats and newborns
the mothers are women sold like fish
A heat wave undulates the tarmac
Seen from the balconies, the sea swallows its waves the wrong
    way
its shells an insult to a bellicose land

**

Rainstorms diluted the country
There is another earth under the earth
another sea beneath the sea say the women who sweep the sea
treasures worthy of a sultan's palace
the slipper of a drowned concubine
throne of an emperor who set his city on fire
Chinese mandarin's tableware
marshal's baton
dog collar
The Mediterranean gives back what we lent it
The sweepers polish their copper and the Alexandrian
    semaphore with the same mixture of ashes and lemon

**

It's snowing on the Mediterranean
The flakes erase the war
The dead no longer tell us their news
the reluctant widows live backwards
daylight breaking into the bomb shelters flows like milk
cats lap it up on the cement then wipe their muzzles on a stain of sunlight

A cat's corpse in the middle of the road
nauseates the sniper
Kneeling on his shadow
he looks at the absent tree, the nest poised in the air
When the war is over
he will go and live in a nest

**

The mothers' voices calling cats and children cross out the clouds
stop the flight of sparrows above the minaret
"Eat, so you'll grow!" they tell the dead children
"Eat, to grow as tall as the ladder"
Luminous bread for the darkened child
Earthy bread for the man who ploughed the sea and sowed his rage between two waves
sure of harvesting enough drowned bodies to stock up for the winter

**

It's snowing in the cannon's mouths and in the chicken-coops
Tossed snow can be eaten raw
The muezzin's call turns into stalactites
Your toes go mad first, the rest follows

The women's calls are a pile of salt on the jetty
The surf brings in shrivelled drowned men and books that have doubled in volume
The wind predicted for tomorrow will separate the pages
and restore to their fate words that cried out in the depths

**

In the church that lost its roof
they burn pebbles in the censer
wash laundry and children in the baptismal font
Tomorrow is Halloween
The killers will fold their evanescent wings to come through the gate

The Mediterranean's days are numbered
With its water drained off
it's a heap of carcasses and fish-bones
Sailors look for its reflection in the clouds
The sniper sees it in his mother's eyes, who knows by his smell that he has killed
"Welcome to the child who replaces the child," she says
and she dresses him as a girl

**

For the women who grew old in the bomb shelters
a country is built above the country
Houses that turn their backs on the waves that tear down the doors
and drag the women clinging to their cries out by their hair

Acknowledgments

The poems beginning
Whether it's true or false
Must you be reminded that you are only what is sad and forgotten
Let's admit that your disappearance was a pretence
Let's admit that you made a bad decision
The shovels peeling away the world's underside make no distinction
Who will find lost time
The woman who isn't in the photo taps her thigh
It's winter in her photographs
How can you weep in a language no longer your own
appeared in *A Public Space* (U.S.)

The Mothers and the Mediterranean
appeared in *The Kenyon Review* (U.S.) and in *PN Review* (U.K.)

The poems beginning
Water down your anger when the river squats on your doormat
The stones in your garden speak louder than the people passing by
Everything speaks to you of departure
Three handfuls of red earth for the shoulder that protected you from the storm
You watch for the moment when dusk makes its way to your table
The faces lined up on the wall invite you to join them
were included in the "Translations" section of *A Stranger's Mirror: New and Selected Poems 1994–2014* by Marilyn Hacker (W.W. Norton, 2015)